Published in 2016
by Igloo Books Ltd
Cottage Farm
Sywell
NN6 0BJ
www.igloobooks.com

Cover images: Main Thinkstock / Getty; all other images Photocuisine UK

LEO002 0316
4 6 8 10 9 7 5 3
ISBN 978-1-78440-685-1

Printed and manufactured in China

Contents

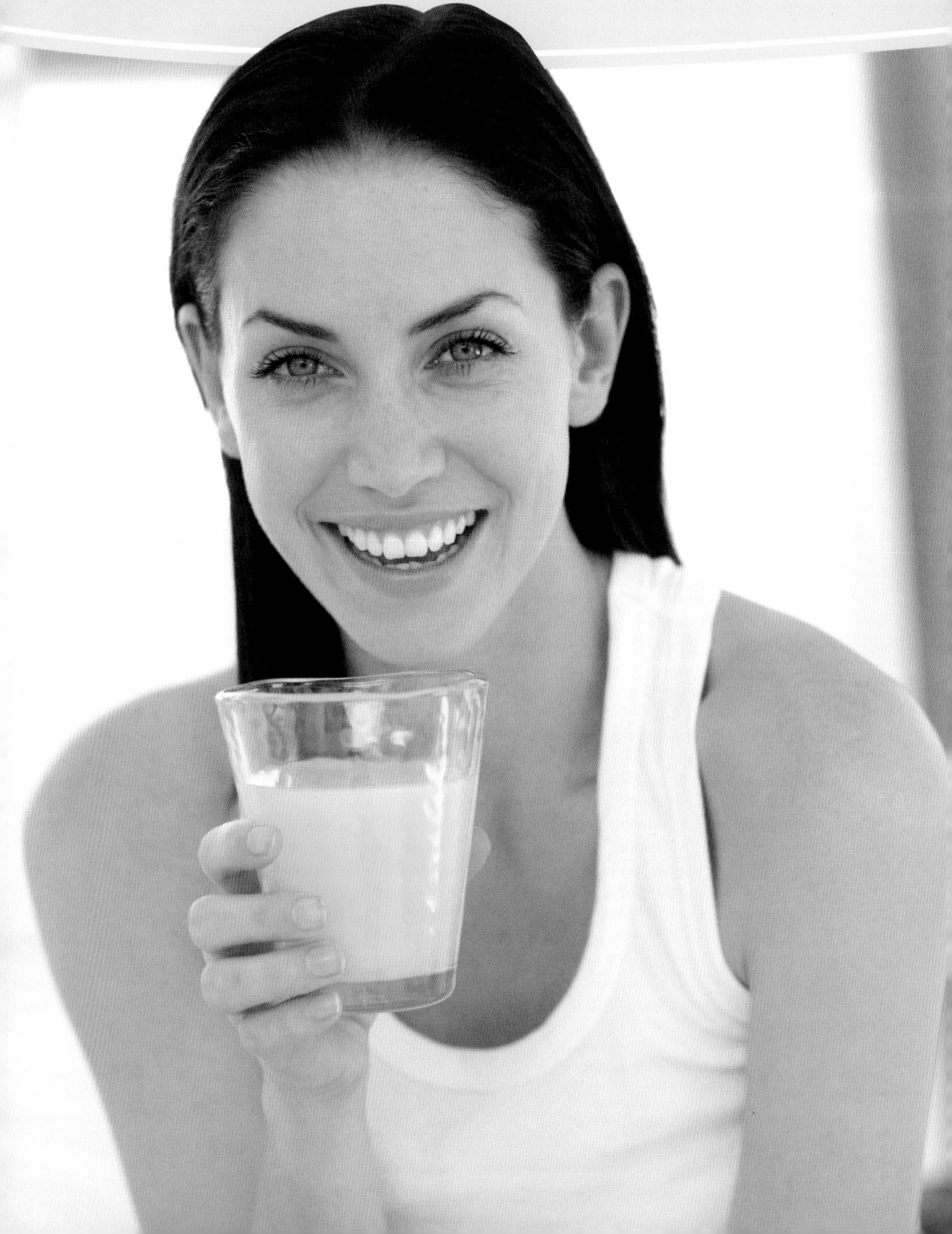

Introduction

What are the benefits of a dairy-free diet? Is it worth the effort? Does your health suffer if you drink milk? Why are so many people nowadays choosing to leave the lactose out of their latte?

For many years, people have actively reduced their consumption of meat products and have sometimes opted to cut out animal products entirely. This is often a decision based on ethics, but more and more it is becoming a matter of health. Milk and other dairy products have well-documented effects on the human body, and a dairy-free diet is often extolled for its benefits to the skin, nasal and aural passages, as well as digestive and immune systems.

Missing out on milk?

Where once a dairy-free diet might have simply meant missing out on milk-based products, that is no longer the case. The advent of milk substitutes and calcium-enriched drinks – and even supplements for people who are lactose-intolerant – means that you can devise a healthy food plan from all the necessary food groups that is both tasty and full of variety. These products are becoming much more widely stocked, so you no longer have to visit specialist health food stores – or avoid high-street coffee shops. Soya hot chocolate, anyone?

What's Milk Made Of?

The main ingredient in milk is water, but it also provides carbohydrate, protein, fat and minerals. There is evidence that a typical supermarket pint can contain less desirable substances, which may be cause for concern.

Natural ingredients

The sweetness in milk comes from lactose, a simple sugar or carbohydrate. Milk also provides protein in the form of casein and whey proteins, as well as vitamins and minerals, including the well-known 'bone maker' calcium. It also has phosphorus, magnesium, potassium, sodium, iodine, selenium, zinc, iron and copper.

The bad stuff

A high proportion of the fats in milk are saturated, which may cause raised cholesterol levels and an increased risk of heart disease. Butter has little or no lactose but is mainly fat, with little nutritional value. However, it's not only the fats that are a worry. Cows' milk naturally contains a variety of hormones and chemicals that stimulate growth in young calves. Whether or not these ingredients are actually bad for humans is the subject of much debate, and opinions are divided right now.

The good news for dairy-lovers is that organic milk shows fewer traces of these additives, and fans of raw (non-pasteurised) milk claim that it contains higher levels of the beneficial nutrients and bacteria that our bodies need.

Say Goodbye

Some people decide to bid farewell to dairy products to improve their well-being. Dairy products – especially cheese, butter and cream – can contribute hugely to our intake of unhealthy saturated fats. By eliminating these animal by-products, people can significantly reduce their fat intake, which will lower their cholesterol levels and may prevent weight gain. Cutting down on dairy may also help to

get rid of many unwanted symptoms of ill health, both external and internal, as explained in the following pages.

Eating ethically

Some people may choose to maintain their normal eating habits, but gradually incorporate small changes in their diet. One way of doing this is to eliminate various dairy foods each week, so the task of going 'dairy-free' isn't so overwhelming.

Others may choose a more drastic change to their diets: vegetarianism and veganism are growing in popularity, due to their health benefits and concerns with the environment and animal welfare. The concept of veganism was developed from the desire to cut out all animal products from the diet. Rearing animals for food uses vast amounts of resources such as water, fodder crops and pasture land for grazing. Using the land for crops for human consumption instead of animal feed is much more productive and less damaging to the ecosystem.

However, the dairy-free diet can be enjoyed with or without meat products – the choice is yours!

Allergy or Intolerance?

Many people have allergies – more than a quarter of the population are affected to varying degrees. Dairy or milk allergies, however, are thankfully rare. It is much more likely that physical reactions to food are caused by an intolerance to one or more basic ingredient.

A milk allergy is caused by the body's immune system reacting to an element in the milk, usually one of the proteins (casein or whey). It releases antibodies to fight this element, which is seen as unwanted. The symptoms can be the same as they are in many other food allergies, including swelling of the mouth or face, wheezing, a rash and, in very extreme cases, anaphylaxis. They may also mirror the digestive complaints listed on page 15. Allergy sufferers need to be vigilant about avoiding all dairy products, even in tiny amounts.

Different tolerances

Milk intolerances don't involve the immune system. Instead, the body cannot process elements in the milk – sometimes the proteins, but more commonly the lactose. Suffering varies in its intensity. Some people feel discomfort while others may be doubled up with cramps. People also have different thresholds of tolerance. While one person might struggle even to have milk in their tea, others can cope with small amounts now and then.

A poor substitute

Be aware that of the people who are allergic to dairy, up to one-quarter of them also turn out to be allergic to soya. So, swapping to soya milk can reveal new problems. Goats' and sheep's milk contain the same proteins, so may also trigger an allergic reaction.

Are You Intolerant?

The symptoms of dairy intolerance are similar to those of many complaints, so you need to establish what is at the root of the problem. If you suspect that milk is to blame, cut out dairy produce for three weeks and then gradually reintroduce items one at a time, starting with the most innocuous, for example bio yoghurt or hard cheese. Keep a note of your body's response as you slowly begin to try dairy products again. Then see your doctor or a registered dietitian to share the results and get further advice.

Acne

Research suggests that consuming milk and whey products can aggravate acne. Milk products can raise insulin levels and levels of IGF-1, a naturally occurring growth hormone, which can then lead to over-production of sebum, the oily substance that clogs pores.

External signs

Dairy produce has been connected to skin and respiratory complaints, including psoriasis, eczema, hives, asthma and sinusitis. Similarly, it is thought that an excess of dairy in the diet exacerbates glue ear and hay fever. Dairy is said to cause an over-production of mucus, which blocks the passages, and inflammation, which makes the problem worse. The jury is out on how much effect dairy has on this set of problems, but it seems certain that a healthy, vitamin-rich, low-fat diet can improve all of these ailments.

Digestive disorders

The most common symptoms of a digestive problem include some, but probably not all, of the following: bloating, excess gas (flatulence), diarrhoea, constipation (children are often affected this way), stomach cramps, nausea, swollen ankles and puffy or dark-circled eyes. These problems may be caused by indigestible lactose remaining in the gut. It begins to ferment, which in turn leads to varying degrees of stomach discomfort, water retention and swelling.

Development disabilities

Some experts are convinced of a link between dairy intolerance and conditions such as autism and Asperger syndrome. In less obvious cases, many children who suffer from lack of energy, aching limbs, distended stomach and mouth ulcers have been found to benefit greatly from the removal of dairy from their diet.

Health Facts – Is It Safe?

Humans are the only creatures on Earth that drink the milk of other species. This realisation may be enough in itself to send you in a dairy-free direction. Globally, around 70 per cent of the adult population is thought to have a dairy intolerance, and the proportion is much higher in some parts of the world.

First food

All mammals are designed to suckle in order to get the nutrition they need to grow. Babies produce an enzyme called lactase, which allows them to break down milk sugars (lactose). However, this enzyme is produced in smaller and smaller quantities as the child (or calf or cub or kitten) grows. The result is that adult mammals cannot easily digest these sugars. Believe it or not, most adult cats are lactose-intolerant, despite the stereotype of a cat lapping up a saucer of milk.

Really rare

True allergic reactions to milk are rare, affecting only one or two per cent of people. Although severe and frightening, they can also change and lessen, with some affected children growing out of their allergy altogether.

This lactose intolerance is exactly the situation for a proportion of weaned humans. Lactase persistence (the continued ability to produce lactase) is genetically determined and is most common in the traditional dairy farming regions of the world – notably, Europe and North America. Lactose intolerance rates are extremely high in cultures that do not rely on dairy produce. Up to 95 per cent of Asian, African and Hispanic people have little or no ability to digest lactose after they are weaned off their mother's milk.

Easy Does It

So, armed with the facts, you may have decided already to do without dairy and feel the benefits. If so, there are some key factors to consider. Some people start slowly, leaving the cheese off their pizza or having spreadless sandwiches. Make a list of all the dairy items you eat regularly and cross off the product you could easily live without. Losing an item or two each week will not seem like a hardship at all.

Read the label

If you are intent on eliminating dairy entirely, you will need to become label-savvy. Check the ingredients list on every item before you buy it – you will be surprised how many foods have 'hidden' milk products in them. (See page 26 for the alternative names you need to watch out for.) However, you will also learn early on that the same product, made by different manufacturers, may or may not contain dairy items. The recipes of some products change and develop, so what could be a no-no one year might find its way back onto your 'yes' list after a time.

Shop around

All products are not created equal! It's purely a matter
of personal taste. If soya milk doesn't tempt your taste
buds, try rice milk or coconut milk. If you don't like
one variety, try another. One brand of almond milk
can taste subtly different from the next, as it may
contain other ingredients, such as vanilla extract,
sugar or natural sweeteners, which will
affect the taste.

Dangerous drinking

Take care when you look for an alternative to milk as a simple thirst-quencher. It's
easy to fall into the trap of replacing milk with drinks that can cause damage in
other ways. Most fruit-based drinks are loaded with sugar and 'empty' calories,
which supply a quick burst of energy but have no nutritional value. Fizzy drinks,
especially caffeinated ones such as cola, are even worse. They may actually
leach minerals from our bones, lowering bone density and increasing the risk of
fractures and osteoporosis.

Added bonuses

Reducing the amount of dairy in your diet has also been shown to help relieve
the symptoms of endometriosis (a condition of the female reproductive system)
by lessening the inflammation of the affected areas caused by dairy foods.
Cutting down on dairy also benefits smokers who are trying to quit, as it helps
to stop the build-up of mucus at the start of the process.

Milk Mates

Many of the recipes in this book leave out any semblance of dairy produce, including milk substitutes. There will be times, though, when you really need a splash of the white stuff – whether it's in your tea, to make a sauce or to pour on your cereal in the morning. So what are the options?

If you are lactose-intolerant, you can simply use lactose-free milk or take lactase tablets before consuming regular dairy produce. The former has added lactase, and both options break down the lactose that your body finds hard to handle. Consult your doctor first, before taking lactase tablets.

Milk substitutes

The most common substitutes for milk are plant-based. Milk can be extracted from many things: soya beans, rice, oats, coconut, quinoa, nuts (almonds, hazelnuts, cobnuts, cashews, brazil nuts) and even potatoes and hemp. Coconut milk has a delicious, distinctive taste and is excellent for cooking.

Soya milk is the most widely available and versatile alternative to cows' milk and it offers about the same amount of protein. However, it has lower levels of digestible calcium than cows' milk, so it is often calcium-enriched when sold in cartons. Soya milk is also made into other products, such as cheese, cream and yoghurt.

Hemp milk is thick and can be grainy. It provides less calcium than cows' milk but has high levels of omega-3 fatty acids, which are good for the heart.

Rice milk is as white as its dairy relative but quite thin, so better for drinking or pouring than for cooking. It is fairly low in protein, as are many nut milks.

Oat milk is low in fat and usually enriched with vitamins and calcium. It has a slightly sweet taste and makes a great drink, as well as offering a good alternative to cows' milk in cooking.

Everything in moderation

Be careful when introducing dairy alternatives, especially as a remedy for certain physical symptoms. Too much of the alternative can overload the system in a new way, leading to similar, negative reactions.

Don't Lose Out

It is important that cutting out dairy from your diet, whether for intolerance issues or general health and lifestyle reasons, does not mean you miss out on vital nutrients. You must be sure that your new regimen replaces the dairy food group with a variety of other nutrient-dense foods.

Milk, thanks to the calcium it contains, has long been linked to having healthy teeth and bones. It is true that children need to build strong bones to serve them in their adult life (when bone production turns to bone deterioration). Calcium is also essential for other areas of body maintenance – namely, blood clotting and nerve and muscle function. Dairy products, however, are by no means the only source of calcium.

Using soya milk and bio yoghurt

Soya milk contains far fewer calories than regular whole milk but around six times less calcium. However, these days it is generally sold fortified with extra calcium. Be sure to shake the carton before you pour – studies have shown that the calcium settles at the bottom, and an unshaken portion of soya milk provides much less calcium than is indicated on the nutrition breakdown. You should also look out for calcium-enriched orange juice.

Try introducing plain bio yoghurt, or good-quality live yoghurt, into your diet. Their long fermentation time means that most of the lactose has already been broken down by the bacteria in the yoghurt, saving your body the work. Natural yoghurt is rich in calcium and available in low-fat varieties. Be wary, though, of long-life or UHT yoghurt – it is no longer 'live', so contains no bacteria. Kefir is a fermented milk product, often in the form of a drink, which may also be easily tolerated because of its lactose-consuming bacteria.

Look, too, for recipes that contain calcium-rich ingredients, such as leafy greens, beans and pulses (more of this on page 30), and snack on nuts to increase your calcium intake. A handful of sesame seeds or a drizzling of molasses on salads, cereals and desserts will provide an additional boost.

The Bones Of It

Calcium is vital for healthy teeth and bones – but it cannot work in isolation. Your body also needs both vitamin D, to help absorb the calcium, and a good amount of weight-bearing exercise.

The bright stuff

Vitamin D is essential for bone health and can also protect against colds and depression. Comparatively few foods contain vitamin D, so you have to find other ways to get it. The very best way is from sunshine – just 20 minutes in the fresh air on a sunny day will do the trick (and make you feel great, too). Don't let your skin burn, and be aware that darker skin needs longer exposure to produce a decent amount of the vitamin. Unfortunately, it has to be direct sunlight – it won't work if you are indoors, even behind a window.

You can buy vitamin D supplements, although there is still some debate about how effective these are. Vitamin D can also be found in oily fish, egg yolks, liver and fortified foods such as breakfast cereal, soya milk and orange juice.

Be active

Bones are made up of living tissue and need to be exercised to keep them strong. Regular exercise in youth will help to increase bone mass, and the right sort of activity will prevent bone loss as you age. Swimming and cycling don't contribute, as they are not 'weight-bearing' exercise. You need to be working against gravity to reap the rewards: tennis, walking, jogging, golf and dancing are all good choices. Resistance exercise such as weight training also helps, and gardening, housework and even lifting the shopping count as well.

Brittle bones

Osteoporosis is a condition that weakens bones, making them more likely to fracture. It affects many people, especially in old age. Bone density is determined in your youth and you reach your maximum bone mass around age 30. After this, bone mass gradually starts to decline.

Milk By Any Other Name

As you embark upon your dairy-free journey, you will need to learn how to spot milk and its relatives, in all of their forms. It may seem obvious to avoid cream, cheese and butter, but watch out, too, for dairy in disguise!

People with a true milk allergy will need to be sure they are not exposed to the wrong products in any form. If you are intolerant, you may be able to get away with small amounts of exposure without drastic consequences. Once tested and diagnosed, you will know whether your body reacts to lactose or to milk proteins. Soon, you will become an expert in reading food labels, but remember that ingredients may change – so, check the packaging every time you buy.

Look for these key dairy giveaway terms in the ingredients listing:

- whey/whey protein/ whey sugar
- hydrolysed whey
- casein/caseinates
- hydrolysed casein
- buttermilk
- ghee
- curds
- crème fraiche
- quark
- rennet
- lactalbumin
- lactose
- milk solids
- lactic acid (E270)
- lactobacillus
- lactoglobulin.

Pre-packaged problems

Many off-the-shelf products contain milk derivatives when you least expect them. Breadcrumbs, batter and butter-basted products are common culprits. Be especially careful when you buy any of the following:

- sausages, ham, turkey/chicken slices, coated fish/chicken products, pizza, pies, pâté

- crisps, dips

- sweets, cakes, biscuits, crackers, ice cream, gelato

- bread, crumpets, muffins, breakfast cereals, pancakes

- stock, gravy, table sauces, salad dressing, cooking sauces

- instant potato

- some beer and wine

- pills and medicines.

To really be sure of what you're eating, cook from scratch!

The good news

Dark chocolate is likely to be lactose-free. Hurrah! The higher the cocoa content, the less likely it is to cause problems – aim for 70 per cent or above. Always be sure to check the label first.

Milk Myths

Mention the 'm' word and you will doubtless find that many people are self-proclaimed nutritionists, with dairy produce a specialist subject. Don't believe all you hear, however…

Whole milk is the worst for lactose intolerance

False. The proportion of lactose in skimmed and semi-skimmed milk is around the same as in whole milk, making the 'lighter' versions no better than full-fat milk.

A dairy-free diet can include eggs and cheese

True – and false, depending on your reasons for being dairy free. Eggs are not classed as dairy – they contain no lactose – so can be eaten if you have an intolerance or allergy, but not if you have chosen a vegan lifestyle. Similarly, hard cheeses such as Edam, Cheddar, Parmesan and Emmental have very little lactose left in them, so may suit those with intolerances.

Goats' milk isn't as bad as cows' milk

Again, it depends. Goats' milk, as well as buffalos' milk and sheep's milk, are obviously from animal sources, and contain both lactose and milk proteins. However, it is thought that these non-cows' milks are digested more completely and so are more easily handled by the body. You may be able to drink goats' milk, depending on your particular allergy or intolerance.

Dairy-free products are no good for cooking with

False – but you have to become substitute-savvy. Some dairy-free spreads and fats can be used in baking, but you will find that your cakes' ability to rise will vary between products. Rice milk can be slightly gritty, coconut milk has a distinctive taste that may not suit some recipes, soya milk is creamy but cannot be whipped, and thinner milks don't always produce great sauces. Likewise, some dairy-free cheeses melt well and are great for pizzas and pasta dishes. Several hard dairy-free cheeses make pretty poor sandwich fillers, but work well in cooking.

Healthy Checklist

It is patently clear that you should not simply remove dairy items from your diet without finding nutrient-rich foods to take their place. Don't despair, though, if you are forced to find alternatives because of an allergy or intolerance – there are so many delicious ingredients just waiting to be discovered!

You have read about the importance of calcium. Fortunately, it is easy to find the mineral in many different foods other than dairy. Choose protein-packed beans – white, kidney and black-eyed – and look for lentils, chickpeas and other pulses and legumes, which will boost both your omega-3s and fibre. Nuts (especially almonds), dates, figs, prunes and dried apricots are great for calcium, too.

Healthy alternatives

One of the best food groups for calcium is leafy greens. Kale, okra, broccoli, watercress, spring greens and pak choi are all excellent vegetables to choose from, although be sure not to overcook them and wipe out any nutritional value.

Look to the sea for more calcium-rich content. If you are not taking the animal-free route, cook with sardines and pilchards, anchovies and tinned salmon – in other words, fish that still contains some bones. You could also try some seaweed! It's full of calcium, fibre and iodine.

Apart from calcium, it is important to ensure that you get enough protein from non-milk foods. Meat and eggs are prime sources, but if you are also cutting them out, try to include vegetarian proteins such as tofu, tempeh and edamame beans. Grains such as quinoa and amaranth are great sources and very versatile. Nuts and nut butter (look for low-sugar varieties without hydrogenated oils), and many seeds (sesame, sunflower, poppy, chia and hemp), all up your protein intake.

Eating out

Finding the right restaurant can be tricky, but keep cultural differences in mind for a dairy-free experience. The lack of milk in Japanese and South-east Asian cuisines makes their restaurants a good bet for your dairy-free requirements.

Breakfasts and Brunches

Now you're armed with much more information, it's time to make a start. Get up and go with a delicious, tasty, dairy-free meal that's balanced and nutritious. Make sure you keep things varied – your diet will suffer if you stick to the same set of breakfasts and mid-morning snacks.

Planning and preparation are vital, so use the shopping lists and meal planners at the back of the book to think ahead. Make sure you have all you need to get started. You don't want to roll out of bed in the morning and not have the key ingredients for your first dairy-free meal!

Don't forget the importance of exercise for a healthy lifestyle, strong bones, vitamin D boost and general well-being. Prepare a breakfast that takes your fancy, then head out for an early morning jog, walk or gym class before coming home to refuel in the best possible way.

Mushroom-baked Eggs

Serves: 4
Preparation time: 10 minutes
Cooking time: 15 minutes
Calories/serving: 286

Ingredients

3 tbsp olive oil

2 cloves of garlic, minced

450 g / 1 lb / 6 cups mixed wild mushrooms

100 g / 3 ½ oz / 1 cup dairy-free cheese, grated

4 large eggs

salt and freshly ground black pepper

Method

1. Preheat the oven to 180°C (160°C fan) / 350F / gas 4. Heat the oil in a large sauté pan set over a moderate heat until hot.

2. Add the garlic and sauté for 30 seconds, then add the mushrooms. Continue to cook for a further 4–5 minutes until softened.

3. Spoon the mushrooms into individual baking dishes and top with the cheese. Crack over an egg and season with salt and pepper before transferring to the oven.

4. Bake for 4–5 minutes until the eggs are set before serving.

Fruity Quinoa Porridge

Serves: 4
Preparation time: 10 minutes
Cooking time: 15 minutes
Calories/serving: 400

Ingredients

200 g / 7 oz / 1 cup quinoa, rinsed and drained

375 ml / 13 fl. oz / 1 ½ cups unsweetened almond milk

250 ml / 9 fl. oz / 1 cup water

3 tbsp agave nectar

150 g / 5 oz / ⅔ cup blackcurrant jam (jelly)

110 g / 4 oz / ¾ cup blackberries

½ lemon, juiced

2 tbsp shelled pistachios, chopped

Method

1. Place the quinoa, almond milk, water and agave nectar in a large saucepan and bring to a simmer over a moderate heat.

2. Reduce to a gentle simmer and cook for 10–12 minutes until the porridge is thick and creamy.

3. Warm together the blackcurrant jam, blackberries and lemon juice in a small saucepan.

4. Spoon the porridge into bowls and top with the fruity jam and pistachios before serving.

Apple French Toast

Serves: 4
Preparation time: 10 minutes
Cooking time: 20 minutes
Calories/serving: 501

Ingredients

3 tbsp coconut oil

2 large Golden Delicious apples, cored and cut into wedges

75 g / 3 oz / ⅓ cup caster (superfine) sugar

4 large eggs

500 ml / 18 fl. oz / 2 cups soya milk

½ tsp vanilla extract

1 large loaf of white sandwich bread, cut into 8 slices

Method

1. Preheat the oven to 190°C (170°C fan) / 375F / gas 5. Melt the coconut oil in a heatproof sauté pan set over a moderate heat.

2. Add the apples and half of the sugar, then toss well and cook for 3–4 minutes until softened.

3. Remove the apple to a plate, then whisk together the eggs and milk with the remaining sugar and the vanilla extract.

4. Dip the slices of bread into the egg mixture before covering the base of the pan with half. Top with apple before covering with another layer of bread.

5. Transfer the pan to the oven to cook for 8–10 minutes until the bread is golden. Leave to stand before serving.

Chunky Cereal Bars

Serves: 8
Preparation time: 5 minutes
Cooking time: 55–60 minutes
Calories/serving: 442

Ingredients

175 g / 6 oz / ¾ cup extra virgin coconut oil
175 g / 6 oz / ¾ cup golden syrup
350 g / 12 oz / 3 cups rolled oats
110 g / 4 oz / ⅔ cup raisins
a pinch of salt

Method

1. Preheat the oven to 160°C (140°C fan) / 325F / gas 3 and line a 18 cm (7 in) square tin with greaseproof paper.

2. Melt together the coconut oil and golden syrup in a saucepan set over a moderate heat.

3. Stir in the oats, raisins and salt, mixing as thoroughly as possible.

4. Spoon the mixture into the lined tin and tap it on a flat surface a few times to help the mixture settle.

5. Bake for 40–45 minutes until golden-brown on top and set. Remove to a wire rack to cool before cutting and serving.

Stewed Fruit

Serves: 4
Preparation time: 5 minutes
Cooking time: 15 minutes
Calories/serving: 147

Ingredients

600 g / 1 lb 5 oz / 4 cups Bramley apples,
    peeled, cored and roughly chopped

300 g / 10 ½ oz / 2 cups blackberries

55 g / 2 oz / ¼ cup caster (superfine) sugar

2 tbsp hot water

½ lemon, juiced

Method

1. Combine the fruit, sugar, water and lemon
   juice in a large saucepan.

2. Cover and cook over a low heat for 12–15
   minutes until soft and juicy.

3. Leave to cool a little before spooning into
   glasses. Serve warm or cold.

Strawberry Smoothie

Serves: 4
Preparation time: 10 minutes
Calories/serving: 142

Ingredients

250 g / 9 oz / 1 cup dairy-free
coconut milk yoghurt

250 ml / 9 fl. oz / 1 cup unsweetened
almond milk

125 g / 4 ½ oz / ½ cup crushed ice

2 tbsp agave nectar

300 g / 10 ½ oz / 2 cups strawberries,
hulled and chopped

a few mint leaves, to garnish

Method

1. Combine all the ingredients apart from the
mint in a food processor.

2. Blitz until smooth, then divide between
glasses and garnish with mint before
serving.

Salmon and Egg Galettes

Serves: 4
Preparation time:
10 minutes plus chilling
Cooking time: 40 minutes
Calories/serving: 228

Ingredients

300 ml / 10 ½ fl. oz / 1 ¼ cups almond milk
6 small eggs
a small bunch of chives, finely chopped
100 g / 3 ½ oz / ⅔ cup buckwheat flour
3 tbsp sunflower oil
110 g / 4 oz / ⅔ cup smoked salmon slices
½ lemon, juiced
salt and freshly ground black pepper

Method

1. Whisk together 225 ml / 8 fl. oz / ¾ cup of the milk with 2 eggs, a little seasoning and the chives in a mixing bowl.

2. Add the flour and gradually whisk into a smooth batter; cover and chill for 30 minutes.

3. Grease a small frying pan with oil, then add a generous tablespoon of batter. Cook briefly until blistered, then flip and cook the other side for 1 minute. Keep warm.

4. Whisk the remaining milk with the remaining eggs and a little seasoning.

5. Heat a saucepan over a medium heat until hot and cook the eggs until softly scrambled.

6. Dress the salmon with lemon juice and serve over the galettes and eggs.

Spiced Oat Porridge

Serves: 4
Preparation time: 5 minutes
Cooking time: 10 minutes
Calories/serving: 331

Ingredients

150 g / 5 oz / 1 ½ cups rolled oats

450 ml / 16 fl. oz / 2 cups oat milk

375 ml / 13 fl. oz / 1 ½ cups cold water

2 small gala or Fuji apples, cored and chopped

55 g / 2 oz / ½ cup walnuts, crushed

2 tsp ground cinnamon

Method

1. Combine the oats, milk and water in a large, heavy-based saucepan set over a medium heat.

2. Bring the liquid to a simmer and cook steadily for 6–7 minutes until thickened and creamy.

3. Spoon into bowls and top with chopped apple, crushed walnuts and a sprinkling of ground cinnamon before serving.

Redcurrant Panettone

Serves: 6
Preparation time:
20 minutes plus proving
Cooking time: 45–50 minutes
Calories/serving: 471

Ingredients

1 tbsp dry active yeast

75 ml / 3 fl. oz / ⅓ cup lukewarm water

55 g / 2 oz / ¼ cup golden caster (superfine) sugar

3 large eggs

2 tbsp redcurrants

2 tbsp mixed citrus peel

75 g / 3 oz / ½ cup raisins

110 g / 4 oz / ½ cup coconut oil

300 g / 10 ½ oz / 2 cups plain (all-purpose) flour, plus extra

redcurrant jelly, to serve

Method

1. Dissolve the yeast in the water in a large bowl; mix in the sugar, eggs, redcurrants, mixed citrus peel, raisins and coconut oil.

2. Gradually add the flour to the bowl, stirring well, until you have a soft dough.

3. Turn out onto a floured surface and knead until smooth and elastic.

4. Place the dough in an oiled bowl. Cover loosely and leave to prove until doubled in size, for 40–45 minutes.

5. Knock back the dough and shape into a small round cake tin, before leaving to prove again for 40–45 minutes.

6. Preheat the oven to 180°C (160°C fan) / 350F / gas 4 and bake for 45–50 minutes until golden and risen before serving with redcurrant jelly.

Mushroom Frittata

Serves: 4
Preparation time: 10 minutes
Cooking time: 20 minutes
Calories/serving: 207

Ingredients

8 large eggs

2 large egg whites

250 ml / 9 fl. oz / 1 cup oat milk

2 tbsp sunflower oil

1 green chilli (chili), finely chopped

225 g / 8 oz / 1 ½ cups mixed wild
  mushrooms

a few chives, to garnish

salt and freshly ground black pepper

Method

1. Preheat the oven to 180°C (160°C fan) /
   350F / gas 4. Whisk together the eggs, egg
   whites, milk and seasoning in a large jug.

2. Heat the oil in a sauté pan set over
   a moderate heat until hot. Add the chilli
   and sauté for 1 minute before adding
   the mushrooms.

3. Cook for 5–6 minutes until softened, then
   season with salt and pepper.

4. Pour over the egg mixture and leave to set
   for 1 minute before transferring to the oven.
   Bake for 10–12 minutes until puffed
   and golden.

5. Remove and leave to cool, then turn out
   and serve with a garnish of chives.

Blackberry Muffins

Makes: 8
Preparation time: 5–10 minutes
Cooking time: 18–22 minutes
Calories/serving: 155

Ingredients

110 g / 4 oz / ⅔ cup self-raising flour, sifted
110 g / 4 oz / ½ cup caster (superfine) sugar
110 ml / 4 fl. oz / ½ cup sunflower oil
2 large eggs
1 tsp bicarbonate of (baking) soda
a pinch of salt
225 g / 8 oz / 1 ½ cups blackberries
2 tbsp dairy-free coconut milk yoghurt
½ lemon, juiced

Method

1. Preheat the oven to 180°C (160°C fan) / 350F / gas 4. Line a 12-hole muffin tray with
8 paper cases.

2. Combine the flour, sugar, oil, eggs, bicarbonate of soda, and salt in a large mixing bowl and beat using an electric mixer until just combined.

3. Fold through the blackberries, coconut yoghurt and lemon juice until just combined.

4. Spoon into the muffin cases and bake for 18–22 minutes until risen and a toothpick comes out clean from their centres.

5. Remove to a wire rack to cool before serving.

Thyme-poached Eggs

Serves: 4
Preparation time: 5 minutes
Cooking time: 10 minutes
Calories/serving: 127

Ingredients

a few sprigs of thyme

1 tbsp white wine vinegar

8 medium eggs

salt and freshly ground mixed peppercorns

Method

1. Bring a large saucepan of water to a steady simmer. Add some of the thyme and the vinegar.

2. Crack the eggs into cups. Poach 4 at a time for 3 minutes before removing with a slotted spoon to drain on kitchen paper.

3. Serve the eggs with the remaining thyme and seasoned with salt and freshly ground pepper.

Grapefruit Detox Juice

Serves: 4
Preparation time: 10–15 minutes
Calories/serving: 197

Ingredients

4 large carrots, peeled and chopped

2 apples, cored and chopped

2 white grapefruit, juiced

2 ruby red grapefruit, juiced

250 ml / 9 fl. oz / 1 cup almond milk

250 g / 9 oz / 1 cup crushed ice

Method

1. Pass the carrots and apples through a juicer. Collect the juice and combine with the grapefruit juices, almond milk and ice in a food processor or blender.

2. Blitz until smooth, then pour into glasses and serve.

Stuffed Button Mushrooms

Serves: 4
Preparation time: 15 minutes
Cooking time: 30–35 minutes
Calories/serving: 298

Ingredients

1 tbsp dairy-free sunflower spread

8 rashers of streaky bacon, finely chopped

1 shallot, finely chopped

2 cloves of garlic

4 small sticks of celery, peeled and finely diced

75 g / 3 oz / ½ cup sun-dried tomatoes in oil, drained and chopped

a few sprigs of thyme, chopped

12 large button mushrooms

55 ml / 2 fl. oz / ¼ cup olive oil

salt and freshly ground black pepper

Method

1. Preheat the oven to 190°C (170°C fan) / 375F / gas 5. Melt the butter in a sauté pan set over a moderate heat until hot.

2. Add the bacon and fry for 2–3 minutes before adding the shallot, garlic, celery, sun-dried tomato and a little salt; continue to fry for 4–5 minutes until golden.

3. Add the thyme and adjust the seasoning to taste. Spoon the mixture into the upturned mushrooms, then place in a baking dish.

4. Drizzle with olive oil and roast for 20–25 minutes until the mushrooms are lightly browned.

Lunches and Light Bites

Embracing a new diet can be daunting, especially when you have to forget old classics. If you're used to grabbing a cheese sandwich or cream cheese bagel, it may take a while before you're satisfied with the dairy-free substitutes.

Don't despair – experiment instead with tasty new recipes. There are many soups and snacks that don't go anywhere near a dairy ingredient but will boost your intake of fresh vegetables beyond the five-a-day target.

When you first begin to cook dairy-free, set aside time at the weekend or in the evening to cook a few lunchtime recipes and see which you like the best. Then you can prepare and freeze them in individual portions, ready to grab and go in the morning. Treat yourself to a funky lunchbox and you'll be the envy of anyone who's about to tackle a soggy sandwich or a boring baguette!

Steamed Cod Salad

Serves: 4
Preparation time: 10–15 minutes
Cooking time: 15–20 minutes
Calories/serving: 258

Ingredients

4 x 175 g / 6 oz cod fillets, pin-boned
2 tbsp olive oil
150 g / 5 oz / 3 cups mixed leaf salad
a small handful of chive stalks, halved
75 g / 3 oz / 1 cup radishes, thinly sliced
½ small white cabbage, shredded
1 large onion, finely sliced into rings
1 lemon, sliced
salt and freshly ground black pepper

Method

1. Place the cod fillets in a steaming basket; drizzle with olive oil and season with plenty of salt and pepper.

2. Cover the basket with a lid and place over a half-filled saucepan of simmering water.

3. Cook for 12–16 minutes until the cod feels firm yet slightly springy to the touch.

4. Toss the salad with half of the chives, the radish and a little salt and pepper. Preheat the grill to hot.

5. Top the steamed cod fillets with slices of onion and lemon and flash under the grill for 2 minutes.

6. Serve the fish over the salad and garnish with the remaining chives before serving.

Chicken Yakitori Salad

Serves: 4
Preparation time:
15 minutes plus marinating
Cooking time: 10 minutes
Calories/serving: 181

Ingredients

55 ml / 2 fl. oz / ¼ cup mirin

75 ml / 3 fl. oz / ⅓ cup light soy sauce

4 skinless chicken breasts, diced

8 wooden skewers, soaked in cold water for 15 minutes beforehand

freshly ground mixed peppercorns

½ Galia melon

1 red pepper, deseeded and finely diced

2 kiwi fruit, peeled and diced

150 g / 5 oz / 3 cups mixed leaf salad

a small bunch of mint leaves, picked

Method

1. Whisk together the mirin and soy sauce in a bowl. Add half to the diced chicken in a separate bowl and stir well to coat.

2. Leave to marinate for 15 minutes. Preheat the grill to hot.

3. Thread the marinated chicken onto the skewers. Arrange on a grilling tray and season with freshly ground pepper.

4. Grill for 7–8 minutes, turning occasionally, until golden and firm to the touch.

5. Use a melon baller to scoop out balls of melon; toss with the pepper, kiwi fruit, mixed leaf salad and mint leaves.

6. Serve the yakitori chicken skewers with the salad on the side. Use the remaining marinade for dipping.

Orange Fennel Salad

Serves: 4
Preparation time: 10 minutes
Cooking time: 10 minutes
Calories/serving: 189

Ingredients

4 large carrots, peeled and cut into batons

4 fennel bulbs, halved

1 lemon, juiced

2 gem lettuce, shredded

flaked sea salt and freshly ground
  black pepper

2 large oranges, peeled and segmented

3 tbsp pine nuts

Method

1. Cook the carrots in a large saucepan of salted, boiling water for 6–8 minutes until tender, then drain and refresh in iced water.

2. Toss the fennel with the lemon juice, gem lettuce, salt and pepper before arranging in serving bowls.

3. Top with orange segments, carrot, pine nuts and a little more seasoning.

Salmon Steak Salad

Serves: 4
Preparation time: 10–15 minutes
Cooking time: 10 minutes
Calories/serving: 405

Ingredients

4 x 150 g / 5 oz salmon steaks

2 tbsp olive oil

1 large head of romanesco cauliflower, prepared into small florets

1 small head of broccoli, prepared into small florets

150 g / 5 oz / 3 cups lamb's lettuce

a small handful of rocket (arugula)

2 tbsp cashews

2 tbsp pecans

salt and freshly ground black pepper

Method

1. Preheat the oven to 220°C (200°C fan) / 425F / gas 7. Sit the salmon on a baking tray and drizzle with olive oil before seasoning with salt and pepper.

2. Roast for 8–10 minutes until firm to the touch. Meanwhile, cook the two kinds of broccoli in a large saucepan of salted, boiling water for 6–8 minutes until tender.

3. Drain and refresh in iced water, then drain and dry well before tossing with the lamb's lettuce and rocket.

4. Arrange on plates and top with the salmon steaks and nuts before serving.

Tofu Sprout Salad

Serves: 4
Preparation time: 5 minutes
Calories/serving: 141

Ingredients

450 g / 1 lb / 3 cups firm tofu, cubed
2 tbsp olive oil
salt and freshly ground black pepper
150 g / 5 oz / 6 cups alfalfa sprouts
a small bunch of micro salad, to garnish

Method

1. Dress the tofu cubes with olive oil and season with salt and pepper.

2. Toss with the sprouts and serve in bowls, garnished with micro salad.

Vegetable Carpaccio

Serves: 4
Preparation time: 10 minutes
Calories/serving: 138

Ingredients

150 g / 5 oz / 2 cups radishes, sliced

4 large cooked beetroot

2 tbsp extra virgin olive oil

2 tbsp sunflower seeds

2 tbsp rolled oats, lightly toasted

a small bunch of chervil, roughly chopped

salt and freshly ground black pepper

Method

1. Thinly slice the radish and beetroot on a mandolin, then overlap slices of the beetroot on plates.

2. Dress with a little olive oil before topping with slices of radish.

3. Garnish with sunflower seeds, oats, chervil and a little salt and pepper.

4. Serve cold for best results.

Chicken Asparagus Salad

Serves: 4
Preparation time: 10–15 minutes
Cooking time: 25–30 minutes
Calories/serving: 279

Ingredients

4 skinless chicken breasts

2 tbsp sunflower oil

2 wholemeal pitta breads, split in half horizontally

250 g / 9 oz / 2 cups asparagus spears, woody ends removed

1 medium red onion, finely sliced

150 g / 5 oz / 3 cups tatsoi and/or mizuna leaves

2 tbsp extra virgin olive oil

½ lemon, juiced

salt and freshly ground black pepper

Method

1. Preheat the grill to hot. Brush the chicken with oil and season, then arrange on a tray.

2. Grill for 16–20 minutes, turning occasionally, until cooked through. Remove from the tray and leave to rest to one side, covered loosely.

3. Grill the pitta bread on the tray until lightly charred, then remove.

4. Blanch the asparagus spears in a saucepan of salted, boiling water for 2 minutes. Drain and refresh in iced water, then cut in half.

5. Toss the red onion, asparagus and salad leaves with extra virgin olive oil, lemon juice, salt and pepper.

6. Cut the pitta bread and arrange on serving plates before topping with the salad; cut the chicken and serve on top.

Crisp Fennel Salad

Serves: 4
Preparation time: 10 minutes
Cooking time: 5 minutes
Calories/serving: 176

Ingredients

1 tsp Dijon mustard
1 tbsp white wine vinegar
a pinch of caster (superfine) sugar
salt and freshly ground black pepper
75 ml / 3 fl. oz / ⅓ cup sunflower oil
8 quail's eggs
4 fennel bulbs
2 large Granny Smith apples, cored
100 g / 3 ½ oz / 1 ⅓ cups radish

Method

1. Whisk together the mustard, vinegar, sugar and seasoning in a small bowl, then slowly whisk in the oil until thickened.

2. Cook the eggs in a large saucepan of boiling water for 3 minutes. Drain and refresh in iced water before peeling and cutting in half.

3. Trim the fronds from the fennel and reserve as a garnish; thinly slice the bulbs on a mandolin.

4. Thinly slice the apples and radish before tossing with the fennel and a little dressing.

5. Spoon the salad into bowls and serve with the eggs, more dressing and a garnish of fennel fronds and black pepper.

Seafood Salad

Serves: 4
Preparation time: 10–15 minutes
Cooking time: 5 minutes
Calories/serving: 253

Ingredients

100 g / 3 ½ oz / 1 cup samphire

150 g / 5 oz / 1 cup cooked brown shrimp

150 g / 5 oz / 1 cup cooked prawns
(shrimp), peeled

100 g / 3 ½ oz / ⅔ cup mussel meat

125 g / 4 ½ oz / ¾ cup cherry
tomatoes, halved

200 g / 7 oz / 1 ⅓ cups mixed leaf salad

200 g / 7 oz / 1 cup canned pineapple
chunks, drained

100 g / 3 ½ oz / ½ cup canned
sweetcorn, drained

a small handful of micro salad, to garnish

multigrain bread, to serve

salt and freshly ground black pepper

Method

1. Cook the samphire in a large saucepan of
   salted, boiling water for 2–3 minutes until
   tender. Drain and refresh in iced water.

2. Toss the samphire with the remaining
   ingredients and spoon into serving bowls.

3. Serve with slices of bread on the side.

Beef Fillet Salad

Serves: 4
Preparation time: 10 minutes
Cooking time: 15 minutes
Calories/serving: 223

Ingredients

2 tbsp sunflower oil

450 g / 1 lb piece of beef fillet, trimmed

150 g / 5 oz / 1 cup mixed cherry
   tomatoes, quartered

100 g / 3 ½ oz / 2 cups baby
   spinach, washed

a few sprigs of mint, chopped

salt and freshly ground black pepper

Method

1. Place a heavy-based frying pan over a
   moderate heat until hot. Add the oil and
   season the beef generously.

2. Carefully lower the beef fillet into the hot oil
   and leave untouched for 3–4 minutes until
   a crust starts to form underneath.

3. Flip the fillet and cook for a further 3–5
   minutes depending on your preferred
   cooking degree.

4. Remove from the pan and leave to rest,
   covered loosely with aluminium foil, for at
   least 5 minutes.

5. Arrange the cherry tomatoes, spinach and
   mint on serving plates; slice the steak and
   serve in stacks next to the salad.

Crunchy Chicken Salad

Serves: 4
Preparation time: 10–15 minutes
Cooking time: 10 minutes
Calories/serving: 205

Ingredients

4 skinless chicken breasts, cut into strips
55 ml / 2 fl. oz / ¼ cup sunflower oil
1 red cabbage, shredded
75 g / 3 oz / 1 cup radishes, sliced
2 small gala apples, cored and thinly sliced
75 g / 3 oz / 1 ½ cups lamb's lettuce
a small bunch of chives, finely chopped
salt and freshly ground black pepper

Method

1. Preheat the grill to hot. Brush the chicken strips with oil and season with salt and pepper.

2. Arrange on a tray and grill for 8–10 minutes, turning once halfway through, until golden and cooked through.

3. Meanwhile, toss together the cabbage, radish, apple, lamb's lettuce and chives in a large mixing bowl. Season with salt and pepper.

4. Divide the salad between plates and top with the grilled chicken before serving.

Fruity Chicken Salad

Serves: 4
Preparation time: 15 minutes
Cooking time: 20 minutes
Calories/serving: 275

Ingredients

2 large chicken breasts, sliced

2 tbsp sunflower oil

3 tbsp olive oil

300 g / 10 ½ oz / 2 cups apricots,
  pitted and sliced

1 shallot, finely sliced

100 g / 3 ½ oz / 2 cups watercress

3 tbsp flaked (slivered) almonds

3 tbsp balsamic vinegar

1 tsp ground mixed peppercorns

Method

1. Preheat a griddle pan over a moderate heat until hot. Brush the chicken with sunflower oil and season with salt and pepper.

2. Griddle for 8–10 minutes until cooked through; remove from the pan.

3. Brush the apricots with 1 tbsp of olive oil and season, then griddle in the pan for 4–5 minutes until lightly charred.

4. Toss the chicken with the apricots, shallot, watercress and almonds. Mix the remaining olive oil with balsamic vinegar and the mixed peppercorns and serve in pots on the side.

Chinese Cabbage Salad

Serves: 4
Preparation time: 10–15 minutes
Calories/serving: 135

Ingredients

55 ml / 2 fl. oz / ¼ cup groundnut oil

2 tbsp rice wine vinegar

2 tbsp dark soy sauce

1 tsp caster (superfine) sugar

2 small heads of Chinese cabbage, chopped

4 large carrots, peeled and grated

a small bunch of mint, chopped

salt and freshly ground black pepper

Method

1. Whisk together the oil, vinegar, soy sauce and sugar in a small mixing bowl until the sugar dissolves.

2. Combine the chopped cabbage and carrot in a large mixing bowl. Add the dressing and mint, tossing well to coat.

3. Season with salt and pepper, then serve in bowls.

Warm Samphire Salad

Serves: 4
Preparation time: 10 minutes
Cooking time: 25–30 minutes
Calories/serving: 164

Ingredients

300 g / 10 ½ oz / 2 cups cherry tomatoes
on the vine

2 small courgettes (zucchini), sliced

55 ml / 2 fl. oz / ¼ cup olive oil

225 g / 8 oz / 2 cups samphire

salt and freshly ground black pepper

Method

1. Preheat the oven to 200°C (180°C fan) /
   400F / gas 6. Toss the cherry tomatoes
   and sliced courgettes with olive oil and
   seasoning.

2. Spread out over a large baking tray and
   roast for 20–25 minutes.

3. Cook the samphire in a large saucepan
   of salted, boiling water for 2–3 minutes
   until tender.

4. Drain and toss with the roasted vegetables
   before serving.

Main Meals

Cooking the main meal of the day can be surprisingly easy on a dairy-free diet. Numerous ingredients are not dairy related at all, so your only concern is using dairy-free fats for frying and roasting. Preparing a meal from scratch, with fresh ingredients that you have assembled yourself, eliminates any concerns about the contents of pre-packaged and processed food.

Any good cook will draw up a meal plan before hosting a dinner party or cooking for the week, and the dairy-free chef is no different. Work out what you want to serve, based on a good balance of main ingredients, spices and herbs. The canny cook will stick to a foolproof list of meat-free Monday, fish on Tuesday, chicken on Wednesday or similar, making it easier to choose a recipe for each day.

Don't forget to look to other cultures for inspiration. It also means you get to avoid the menu minefield – if you can't be sure that your local Thai or Indian restaurant has dairy-free choices, simply cook a curry yourself!

Turkey and Grain Salad

Serves: 4
Preparation time: 10 minutes
Cooking time: 20–25 minutes
Calories/serving: 345

Ingredients

1 tsp Dijon mustard

2 tbsp white wine vinegar

100 ml / 3 fl. oz / ½ cup sunflower oil

150 g / 5 oz / ⅔ cup giant couscous

2 tbsp coconut oil

1 onion, finely chopped

100 g / 3 ½ oz / 1 cup mixed wild mushrooms, roughly chopped

100 g / 3 ½ oz / 2 cups baby spinach, washed

400 g / 14 oz / 2 ⅔ cups roast turkey breast, sliced

salt and freshly ground pepper

Method

1. Whisk together the mustard, vinegar and seasoning in a small bowl. Whisk in the oil in a slow, steady stream until you have a thickened dressing.

2. Place the couscous in a large saucepan and cover with plenty of water. Simmer over a moderate heat and cook steadily for 4–5 minutes until tender before draining.

3. Melt the coconut oil in a sauté pan set over a medium heat, then add the onion, mushrooms and a little salt and sweat for 6–8 minutes until softened.

4. Stir in the cooked couscous and season to taste. Spoon onto plates.

5. Serve with the spinach, slices of turkey and dressing spooned around.

Vegetarian Spaghetti Salad

Serves: 4
Preparation time: 10–15 minutes
Cooking time: 15 minutes
Calories/serving: 449

Ingredients

350 g / 12 oz / 3 cups spaghetti

2 tbsp olive oil

225 g / 8 oz / 1 ½ cups pearl onions, peeled and halved

3 cloves black or smoked garlic, sliced

150 g / 5 oz / 1 cup cherry tomatoes, halved

100 g / 3 ½ oz / ⅔ cup pitted green olives, chopped

a small handful of rocket (arugula)

salt and freshly ground black pepper

Method

1. Cook the spaghetti in a large saucepan of salted, boiling water for 8–10 minutes until 'al dente'.

2. Meanwhile, heat the olive oil in a large saucepan set over a moderate heat until hot. Add the onions, garlic and a little salt, sautéing for 5–6 minutes.

3. Add the cherry tomatoes and olives and continue to cook over a reduced heat for 3 minutes.

4. Drain the pasta well, reserving half a cup of the cooking liquid. Add this to the saucepan and toss well, adding a little of the cooking liquid to loosen as necessary.

5. Stir through the rocket and season to taste before serving.

Seitan Stir-fry

Serves: 4
Preparation time: 15 minutes
Cooking time: 10 minutes
Calories/serving: 203

Ingredients

2 tbsp sunflower oil

450 g / 1 lb / 3 cups seitan, sliced

2 large carrots, peeled and cut into batons

150 g / 5 oz / 1 cup runner beans, sliced

225 g / 8 oz / 2 cups green (string) beans

100 g / 3 ½ oz / ½ cup canned
   sweetcorn, drained

100 g / 3 ½ oz / 2 cups beansprouts

2 tbsp light soy sauce

1 tbsp rice wine vinegar

salt and freshly ground black pepper

Method

1. Heat the oil in a large wok set over a high heat until hot, then add the seitan and stir-fry for 2–3 minutes.

2. Add the carrot, runner beans, green beans and sweetcorn. Cover with a lid and cook over a reduced heat for 2–3 minutes.

3. Remove the cover and add the beansprouts. Continue to stir-fry for 2–3 minutes until the beansprouts start to turn translucent.

4. Season to taste with soy sauce, rice wine vinegar, salt and pepper as necessary before serving.

Seafood Sauerkraut

Serves: 4
Preparation time:
20 minutes plus standing
Cooking time: 20–25 minutes
Calories/serving: 379

Ingredients

1 small white cabbage, shredded

2 eating apples, peeled, cored and grated

½ tsp juniper berries, crushed

150 g / 5 oz / 1 cup mussels, cleaned with beards removed

400 g / 14 oz / 2 cups skinless salmon fillet, cut into 4 even chunks

400 g / 14 oz / 2 cups skinless halibut fillet, cut into 4 even chunks

150 g / 5 oz / 1 cup whole prawns (shrimp)

100 g / 3 ½ oz / ⅔ cup smoked haddock fillet, thinly sliced

500 ml / 18 fl. oz / 2 cups fish stock

a few sprigs of dill, to garnish

salt and freshly ground black pepper

Method

1. Combine the cabbage, apple, juniper berries and 1 tsp of salt in a large casserole dish. Cover and leave for 1 hour.

2. Drain the liquid after 1 hour and place the dish over a medium heat.

3. Cover and sweat for 10–15 minutes, stirring occasionally, until the cabbage starts to soften, then add the seafood and fish and cover with the stock.

4. Bring to boiling point and cover, then reduce to a simmer for 7–8 minutes until the mussels open, the fish is cooked and the prawns are pink and tender.

5. Season to taste, then spoon into shallow serving bowls and garnish with sprigs of dill.

Chicken Curry Kebabs

Serves: 4
Preparation time: 25 minutes
Cooking time: 10–12 minutes
Calories/serving: 264

Ingredients

350 g / 12 oz / 1 ½ cups dairy-free
  coconut milk yoghurt

1 tbsp Madras curry powder

a pinch of Cayenne pepper

salt and freshly ground black pepper.

4 skinless chicken breasts, sliced

4 spring onions (scallions)

½ white cabbage, shredded

2 large carrots, julienned

½ lemon, juiced

8 wooden skewers, soaked in water for 30
  minutes beforehand

Method

1. Preheat the grill to a moderately hot
   temperature.

2. Whisk together two-thirds of the coconut
   milk yoghurt with the ground spices and
   seasoning. Add the chicken and stir well to
   coat; cover and chill for 15 minutes.

3. Brush the excess marinade off the chicken
   before threading onto skewers; arrange
   on a grilling tray. Grill for 10–12 minutes,
   turning occasionally, until cooked through.

4. Slice three of the spring onions, then add
   to a mixing bowl with the cabbage, carrots,
   lemon juice, remaining coconut milk
   yoghurt and seasoning; stir well to coat.

5. Finely slice the remaining spring onion.
   Serve the kebabs over the dressed salad
   with a garnish of finely sliced spring onion.

Thai Bream Stew

Serves: 4
Preparation time: 10–15 minutes
Cooking time: 20 minutes
Calories/serving: 245

Ingredients

1 tbsp sunflower oil

1 tbsp Thai green curry paste

250 g / 9 oz / 2 cups asparagus spears, woody ends removed and chopped

2 red peppers, deseeded and sliced

500 ml / 18 fl. oz / 2 cups fish stock, hot

4 x 150 g / 5 oz sea bream fillets, pin-boned and descaled

a few sprigs of flat-leaf parsley, to garnish

salt and freshly ground black pepper

Method

1. Preheat the oven to 190°C (170°C fan) / 375F / gas 5. Heat the sunflower oil in a large casserole dish set over a moderate heat.

2. Add the curry paste and fry for 1 minute until fragrant before adding the asparagus and pepper.

3. Sauté over a reduced heat for 2–3 minutes, then stir in the stock.

4. Bring to a simmer before positioning the sea bream on top.

5. Season and roast for 10–12 minutes; the flesh should be firm yet slightly springy to the touch.

6. Remove from the oven and season the broth, then serve with a parsley garnish.

Sea Bass Salad

Serves: 4
Preparation time: 15 minutes
Cooking time: 15 minutes
Calories/serving: 293

Ingredients

4 x 175 g / 6 oz skinless sea bass fillets,
  pin-boned

225 g / 8 oz / 2 cups mangetout

1 large cucumber, peeled, halved
  and deseeded

4 large radishes, sliced thinly

2 tbsp white sesame seeds

1 large banana, halved and sliced

2 blood oranges, peeled and segmented

1 red chilli (chili), deseeded and sliced

a few sprigs of coriander (cilantro)

salt and freshly ground black pepper

Method

1. Preheat the oven to 200°C (180°C fan) /
   400F / gas 6 and line a baking tray with
   greaseproof paper.

2. Place the fish on the tray and season with
   salt and pepper. Bake for 10–12 minutes
   until firm yet slightly springy to the touch.

3. Cook the mangetout in a large saucepan
   of salted, boiling water for 2 minutes.
   Drain and refresh in iced water.

4. Slice the cucumber and toss with the
   mangetout and radish and arrange on
   serving plates. Sprinkle with sesame seeds.

5. Top with the sea bass fillets, then toss
   together the banana, orange, chilli and
   coriander and serve in pots on the side.

Mediterranean Tuna Kebabs

Serves: 4
Preparation time: 10–15 minutes
Cooking time: 10 minutes
Calories/serving: 398

Ingredients

600 g / 1 lb 5 oz / 4 cups tuna fillet, cubed

4 slices of prosciutto, folded

2 small vine tomatoes, cored and halved

1 large onion, chopped

55 ml / 2 fl. oz / ¼ cup olive oil

a small bunch of basil leaves, sliced

1 lemon, sliced

4 wooden skewers, soaked in water for 30 minutes beforehand

salt and freshly ground black pepper

Method

1. Preheat the grill to hot. Thread the tuna onto the skewers, alternating with the folded slices of prosciutto, tomato and onion.

2. Brush liberally with olive oil and season with salt and pepper; sprinkle with some of the basil and arrange on a grilling tray.

3. Cook under the grill for 6–8 minutes, turning occasionally, until the tuna is lightly browned all over.

4. Remove from the grill and serve with more basil and lemon slices as a garnish.

Orange Chicken Salad

Serves: 4
Preparation time: 10–15 minutes
Cooking time: 10 minutes
Calories/serving: 219

Ingredients

2 tbsp sunflower oil

2 large skinless chicken breasts

1 small iceberg lettuce, chopped

1 large cucumber, halved and sliced

2 tbsp canned sweetcorn, drained

2 large oranges, peeled and segmented

½ medium cantaloupe melon, balled

1 small white onion, finely sliced into rings

a large handful of cress, to garnish

2 tbsp extra virgin olive oil

salt and freshly ground black pepper

Method

1. Heat the oil in a large frying pan set over a moderate heat until hot. Season the chicken and sauté for 7–8 minutes until golden and cooked through.

2. Toss together the lettuce, cucumber and sweetcorn in a mixing bowl, then arrange in bowls.

3. Top with the orange segments, melon balls, onion, chicken and cress.

4. Drizzle with olive oil before serving.

Steamed Bream Over Rice

Serves: 4
Preparation time: 10–15 minutes
Cooking time: 15 minutes
Calories/serving: 549

Ingredients

8 x 110 g / 4 oz sea bream fillets, pin-boned

8 spring onions (scallions), roughly sliced

250 g / 9 oz / 2 cups mangetout

1 lemon, sliced

3 cm (1 in) piece of root ginger,
    peeled and minced

a pinch of fennel seeds

3 tbsp dark soy sauce

400 g / 14 oz / 2 cups cooked basmati rice

Method

1. Arrange the bream fillets in a large steaming basket. Toss together the spring onions, mangetout, lemon, ginger and fennel seeds before placing over the bream.

2. Spoon over the soy sauce and cover the basket with a lid.

3. Steam over a half-filled saucepan of simmering water for 8–10 minutes until the fish is cooked through.

4. Reheat the rice and spoon into bowls. Top with the vegetables, lemon and bream fillets before serving.

Thai Rice Salad

Serves: 4
Preparation time: 10–15 minutes
Cooking time: 50–55 minutes
Calories/serving: 361

Ingredients

1 l / 1 pint 16 fl. oz / 4 cups vegetable stock

225 g / 8 oz / 1 ½ cups wild rice

2 small heads of broccoli, prepared into florets

225 g / 8 oz / 2 cups petit pois

a small bunch of Thai basil, torn

a small bunch of mint leaves, picked

2 tbsp rice wine vinegar

1 tbsp fish sauce

2 tbsp peanuts, chopped

salt and freshly ground black pepper

Method

1. Bring the stock to the boil in a large saucepan. Stir in the rice and return to the boil, then cover and cook at a simmer for 45–50 minutes until tender.

2. Meanwhile, cook the broccoli in a large saucepan of salted, boiling water for 3–4 minutes, then add the petit pois.

3. Cook for a further 2 minutes, then drain the vegetables and refresh in iced water.

4. Once the rice is cooked, remove from the heat and leave to stand, covered, for 5 minutes, then fluff with a fork.

5. Add the cooked vegetables, herbs, rice wine vinegar, fish sauce, peanuts and seasoning.

6. Spoon into bowls and serve.

Curried Tofu

Serves: 4
Preparation time: 10 minutes
Cooking time: 15 minutes
Calories/serving: 204

Ingredients

3 tbsp sunflower oil

salt and freshly ground black pepper

450 g / 1 lb / 3 cups firm tofu, cubed

1 large onion, finely sliced

225 g / 8 oz / 3 cups mushrooms, sliced

2 tsp Madras curry powder

½ tsp ground cumin

a pinch of Cayenne pepper

a pinch of caster (superfine) sugar

150 ml / 5 fl. oz / ⅔ cup coconut milk

Method

1. Heat the oil in a large frying or sauté pan set over a moderate heat until hot. Season the tofu and fry in the oil for 3–4 minutes until golden.

2. Remove from the pan and add the onion and mushroom with a little salt. Sauté for 3–4 minutes until softened.

3. Sprinkle over the ground spices, Cayenne pepper and sugar, then cook for 1 minute over a reduced heat before returning the tofu to the pan.

4. Cover with the coconut milk and bring to a simmer, then reduce and cook for 2–3 minutes until thickened.

5. Season to taste before serving.

Smoked Chicken Risotto

Serves: 4
Preparation time: 10–15 minutes
Cooking time: 40–50 minutes
Calories/serving: 421

Ingredients

2 tbsp olive oil

1 shallot, finely chopped

2 cloves of garlic, minced

200 g / 7 oz / 1 cup short-grain rice

110 ml / 4 fl. oz / ½ cup dry white wine

1 l / 1 pint 16 fl oz / 4 cups hot chicken stock

2 smoked chicken breasts, chopped

150 g / 5 oz / 1 cup sun-dried tomatoes in oil,
  drained and sliced

a small handful of pea shoots, to garnish

salt and freshly ground black pepper

Method

1. Heat the oil in a large saucepan set over a medium heat until hot. Add the shallot, garlic and a little salt, sweating for 4–5 minutes
until softened.

2. Add the rice and cook for 2–3 minutes, stirring frequently, coating in the oil. Deglaze with the wine and let it reduce by half.

3. Slowly incorporate stock into the rice, ladle by ladle, stirring constantly for 25–35 minutes until the rice absorbs the liquid.

4. Once the rice is plump and tender, stir through the chicken and sun-dried tomato and then season to taste.

5. Spoon into bowls and garnish with pea shoots before serving.

Mediterranean Roast Bream

Serves: 4
Preparation time: 10–15 minutes
Cooking time: 15 minutes
Calories/serving: 584

Ingredients

4 x 200 g / 7 oz sea bream steaks, pin-boned and scaled

55 ml / 2 fl. oz / ¼ cup olive oil

salt and freshly ground black pepper

300 g / 10 ½ oz / 2 cups sun-dried tomatoes in oil

75 g / 3 oz / ½ cup black olives

75 g / 3 oz / ½ cup green olives

a small handful of basil leaves

Method

1. Preheat the oven to 200°C (180°C fan) / 400F / gas 6 and line a roasting tray with a sheet of greaseproof paper.

2. Sit the bream on top of the paper and drizzle with the olive oil, rubbing it in on both the skin and flesh. Season with salt and pepper.

3. Roast for 12–14 minutes until the fish is firm yet slightly springy to the touch.

4. Remove from the oven and serve over a bed of sun-dried tomatoes, garnished with olives and a few basil leaves.

Warm Mushroom Salad

Serves: 4
Preparation time: 10 minutes
Cooking time: 10 minutes
Calories/serving: 149

Ingredients

3 tbsp olive oil
350 g / 12 oz / 4 ½ cups button mushrooms
2 tbsp balsamic vinegar
2 tbsp pine nuts
55 g / 2 oz / ½ cup dairy-free cheese, shaved
a small bunch of basil, picked
salt and freshly ground black pepper

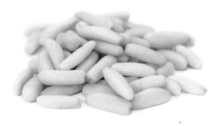

Method

1. Heat the oil in a large sauté pan set over a moderate heat until hot. Add the mushrooms and a little seasoning.

2. Cover with a lid and cook for 2 minutes, then remove the cover and sauté for 5–6 minutes, tossing occasionally, until lightly browned and tender.

3. Add the vinegar and nuts and continue to cook for 1–2 minutes, then season to taste.

4. Serve with a garnish of shaved cheese and basil leaves.

Marinated Scallops

Serves: 4
Preparation time:
15 minutes plus chilling
Cooking time: 15 minutes
Calories/serving: 221

Ingredients

1 lemon

a small bunch of flat-leaf parsley, finely chopped

12 fresh scallops, roe removed

55 ml / 2 fl. oz / ¼ cup olive oil

1 aubergine (eggplant), diced

1 large courgette (zucchini), sliced

200 g / 7 oz / 1 cup passata

salt and freshly ground black pepper

Method

1. Pare the zest from the lemon and finely slice. Juice the lemon into a bowl and add the zest, parsley and seasoning.

2. Whisk well before adding the scallops; coat in the marinade, cover and chill for 15 minutes.

3. Preheat the grill to hot. Toss together the oil, aubergine, courgette and seasoning.

4. Spread out on a tray and grill for 6–8 minutes, turning occasionally, until lightly browned and tender.

5. Remove from the grill and set to one side. Warm the passata in a saucepan.

6. Arrange the scallops on a tray and grill for 2–3 minutes, turning once. Serve the vegetables over the passata with the scallops on top.

Desserts

You may feel that going dairy-free means waving goodbye to the delights of desserts – but that doesn't have to happen. With so many milk and cream substitutes around, there are plenty of cakes, puddings and sweet treats that you can make. And that's not counting all the naturally dairy-free sorbets and fruit puddings you can conjure up.

As mentioned before, different kinds of plant-based milks have their own characteristics, which will affect the taste of a recipe. Some milks have a natural thickness or creaminess that really lends itself to dessert making. The recipes here take that into account, so the hard work has already been done for you. However, you may have your own milks that you rely on for cooking and you will know yourself how well they work in pastries, doughs and batters. Gather together the ingredients for your chosen recipe and if you don't have access to the kind of milk or cream that is listed, use substitute ingredients. Don't be afraid to give it a try!

Stewed Apples

Serves: 4
Preparation time: 10–15 minutes
Cooking time: 15 minutes
Calories/serving: 344

Ingredients

2 tbsp coconut oil

1 kg / 2 lb 4 oz / 6 ⅔ cups Bramley apples,
  peeled, cored and diced

150 g / 5 oz / ⅔ cup caster (superfine) sugar

3 tbsp hot water

a pinch of ground nutmeg

a pinch of ground cinnamon

dairy-free biscuits, to serve

Method

1. Melt the oil in a casserole dish set over a
   medium heat.

2. Add the apples, sugar, water and spices;
   stir well and cover with a lid.

3. Cook over a reduced heat for 12–15
   minutes until very soft.

4. Once soft enough, mash into a rough
   purée. Leave to cool before serving with
   biscuits on the side.

Blueberry Muffins

Makes: 12
Preparation time: 5–10 minutes
Cooking time: 18–22 minutes
Calories/serving: 250

Ingredients

450 g / 1 lb / 3 cups plain (all-purpose) flour, sifted

225 g / 8 oz / 1 cup caster (superfine) sugar

a pinch of salt

1 tsp baking powder

75 g / 3 oz / ⅓ cup sunflower oil

125 g / 4 ½ oz / ½ cup dairy-free coconut milk yoghurt

3 medium eggs

1 tsp vanilla extract

250 g / 9 oz / 2 cups blueberries

Method

1. Preheat the oven to 180°C (160°C fan) / 350F / gas 4 and line a 12-hole muffin tin with paper cases.

2. Combine the flour, sugar, salt and baking powder in a large mixing bowl.

3. In a separate mixing bowl, whisk together the oil, yoghurt, eggs and vanilla extract until smooth.

4. Add to the dry ingredients and mix together until just incorporated, then fold in the blueberries.

5. Spoon into the cupcake cases and bake 18–22 minutes until risen, golden and springy to the touch; a toothpick will come out almost clean from the centres.

6. Remove to a wire rack to cool before serving.

Chocolate Pots

Serves: 4
Preparation time: 5 minutes
Cooking time: 10 minutes
Calories/serving: 257

Ingredients

150 g / 5 oz / 1 cup vegan dark
   chocolate, chopped
2 tbsp agave nectar
250 g / 9 oz / 1 ¼ cups silken tofu, cubed
1 tbsp hot water

Method

1. Melt the chocolate in a heatproof bowl
   set on top of a half-filled saucepan of
   simmering water.

2. Once melted, remove from the heat and
   leave to cool briefly, then scrape into a food
   processor.

3. Add the agave nectar, tofu and water and
   blend until smooth and creamy.

4. Spoon into jars and chill before serving.

Granola and Peaches

Serves: 4
Preparation time: 10 minutes
Cooking time: 25–30 minutes
Calories/serving: 356

Ingredients

2 tbsp sunflower oil

½ tsp vanilla extract

150 g / 5 oz / 1 ½ cups rolled oats

1 tbsp honey

2 tbsp pumpkin seeds

3 tbsp shelled pistachios, chopped

600 g / 1 lb 5 oz / 3 cups canned peaches in syrup

150 g / 5 oz / ⅔ dairy-free coconut milk yoghurt, to serve

Method

1. Preheat the oven to 150°C (130°C fan) / 300F / gas 2 and line a baking tray with greaseproof paper.

2. Mix together the oil, vanilla extract, oats, honey, seeds and pistachios in a large mixing bowl.

3. Spread out evenly on the baking tray and bake for 20–25 minutes until golden brown.

4. Remove to a wire rack to cool, then cut into squares.

5. Serve the peaches in their syrup with yoghurt and granola squares on the side.

Poached Apricots

Serves: 4
Preparation time: 10 minutes
Cooking time: 50–55 minutes
Calories/serving: 307

Ingredients

750 ml / 1 pint 6 fl. oz / 3 cups water

250 ml / 9 fl. oz / 1 cup dry white wine

175 g / 6 oz / 1 cup light brown soft sugar, plus extra for garnishing

2 vanilla pods, split in half lengthwise

600 g / 1lb 5 oz / 4 cups apricots, pitted

a few sprigs of mint, to garnish

Method

1. Combine the water, wine, sugar and vanilla pods in a large saucepan. Bring to boiling point, stirring occasionally, then reduce to a simmer.

2. Add the apricots, stir well and poach for 40–45 minutes until they are very soft.

3. Leave the apricots and syrup to cool slightly before serving in glasses. Garnish with a sprinkling of light brown soft sugar and sprigs of mint.

Strawberry Lavender Soup

Serves: 4
Preparation time: 10 minutes
Cooking time: 15 minutes
Calories/serving: 103

Ingredients

a few sprigs of fresh lavender

750 ml / 1 pint 6 fl. oz / 3 cups cold water

75 g / 3 oz / ⅓ cup caster (superfine) sugar

450 g / 1 lb / 3 cups strawberries,
    hulled and sliced

Method

1. Place the lavender in a saucepan with the water and sugar. Bring to a simmer over a medium heat, stirring occasionally.

2. Once simmering, add the strawberries and cover with a lid. Cook over a reduced heat for 10 minutes until softened, then serve.

Fluffy Fruit Pancakes

Serves: 4
Preparation time: 15 minutes
Cooking time: 20 minutes
Calories/serving: 422

Ingredients

150 g / 5 oz / 1 cup plain (all-purpose) flour
½ tsp baking powder
1 tbsp caster (superfine) sugar
3 small eggs, separated
450 ml / 16 fl. oz / 2 cups almond milk
55 g / 2 oz / ¼ cup coconut oil
2 tbsp flaked (slivered) almonds
250 g / 9 oz / 2 cups raspberries
2 tbsp icing (confectioners') sugar, for dusting

Method

1. Combine the flour, baking powder and caster sugar in a bowl. Whisk three egg yolks and two egg whites with the milk, then whisk into the flour mixture until smooth.

2. Beat the remaining egg whites until softly peaked, then fold into the batter.

3. Melt a teaspoon of coconut oil in a frying pan set over a moderate heat. Crush three-quarters of the raspberries and fold into the batter.

4. Add a ladle of batter to pan and tilt to coat the surface with it; leave to set until golden and puffed, then flip and cook for a further minute.

5. Repeat for the remaining pancakes, then serve in stacks with a garnish of almonds, raspberries and icing sugar.

Spiced Poached Plums

Serves: 4
Preparation time: 5–10 minutes
Cooking time: 30–35 minutes
Calories/serving: 335

Ingredients

1 orange

250 ml / 9 fl. oz / 1 cup port

750 ml / 1 pint 6 fl. oz / 3 cups cold water

150 g / 5 oz / ⅔ cup caster (superfine) sugar

1 tsp cloves

1 cinnamon stick

600 g / 1 lb 5 oz / 4 cups plums

150 g / 5 oz / ⅔ cup dairy-free
    coconut milk yoghurt, to serve

Method

1. Pare the zest from the orange; juice the orange into a saucepan and add the pared zest.

2. Add the port, water, sugar and spices and bring to a simmer, then add the plums.

3. Simmer for 25–30 minutes until the plums are soft to the point of a knife.

4. Leave to cool slightly, then serve with coconut yoghurt on the side.

Luxury Cereal Bars

Serves: 8
Preparation time: 10 minutes
Cooking time: 35–40 minutes
Calories/serving: 368

Ingredients

100 g / 3 ½ oz / ½ cup coconut oil
55 g / 2 oz / ¼ cup almond butter
75 g / 3 oz / ⅓ cup agave nectar
2 large bananas, chopped
60 ml / 2 fl. oz / ¼ cup oat milk
110 g / 4 oz / 1 cup rolled oats
150 g / 5 oz / 1 cup plain (all-purpose) flour
110 g / 4 oz / ⅔ cup raisins

Method

1. Preheat the oven to 180°C (160°C fan) / 350F / gas 4 and line an 18 cm (7 in) square baking tin with greaseproof paper.

2. Melt together the coconut oil, almond butter and agave nectar in a saucepan, then tip into a food processor.

3. Add the banana and oat milk and blend until smooth.

4. Scrape into a bowl and add the oats, flour and raisins. Mix well before spooning into the prepared tin.

5. Bake for 25–30 minutes until golden-brown on top. Remove to a wire rack to cool, then turn out, cut and serve.

Orange Poached Pears

Serves: 4
Preparation time: 10 minutes
Cooking time: 30–35 minutes
Calories/serving: 352

Ingredients

1 l / 1 pint 16 fl. oz / 4 cups cold water

175 g / 6 oz / 1 cup dark brown soft sugar

1 vanilla pod, split lengthwise

110 g / 4 oz / ½ cup orange marmalade

1 orange, zested and juiced

4 Rocha pears, halved and cored

Method

1. Combine the water, sugar, vanilla pod, orange marmalade, orange juice and zest in a saucepan. Bring to boiling point before reducing to a simmer.

2. Add the pear halves and poach for 25–30 minutes until tender.

3. Let the pears and syrup cool a little before serving.

Nutty Baked Apples

Serves: 4
Preparation time: 15 minutes
Cooking time: 35–40 minutes
Calories/serving: 483

Ingredients

150 g / 5 oz / 1 ½ cups rolled oats

75 g / 3 oz / ½ cup raisins

55 g / 2 oz / ½ cup hazelnuts (cobnuts), chopped

1 tbsp almonds, chopped

2 tbsp coconut oil, melted

3 tbsp agave nectar

4 golden delicious apples, cored

2 oranges, peeled and segmented

Method

1. Preheat the oven to 180°C (160°C fan) / 350F / gas 4. Mix together the oats, raisins, nuts, coconut oil and agave nectar in a large mixing bowl.

2. Hollow out the insides of the apples and stuff with the oat mixture.

3. Crush the orange segments before pouring into the base of a heatproof sauté pan. Sit the stuffed apples on top.

4. Bake for 35–40 minutes until the apples are tender to the point of a knife.

5. Remove from the oven and leave to cool slightly before serving.

Spiced Stewed Rhubarb

Serves: 4
Preparation time: 10–15 minutes
Cooking time: 10 minutes
Calories/serving: 385

Ingredients

750 g / 1 lb 10 oz / 6 cups rhubarb, trimmed and cut into chunks

4 whole star anise

½ tsp cardamom pods

3 tbsp hot water

75 ml / 3 fl. oz / ⅓ cup orange juice

110 g / 4 oz / ½ cup caster (superfine) sugar

250 g / 9 oz / 1 cup dairy-free coconut milk yoghurt, to serve

Method

1. Place the rhubarb in a large saucepan with the whole spices, water, orange juice and sugar.

2. Bring to a simmer, cover with a lid and cook over a reduced heat for 5–6 minutes until soft but not mushy.

3. Let the rhubarb cool slightly, then serve with yoghurt on the side.

Summer Fruit Jellies

Serves: 4
Preparation time:
15 minutes plus chilling
Calories/serving: 173

Ingredients

125 g / 4 ½ oz / 1 cup strawberry jelly cubes

600 ml / 1 pint 2 fl. oz / 2 ⅔ cups
  boiling water

250 g / 9 oz / 2 cups raspberries

350 g / 12 oz / 2 ⅓ cups strawberries,
  hulled and chopped

110 g / 4 oz / 1 cup redcurrants

a few sprigs of basil

Method

1. Place the jelly cubes in a jug. Pour over a third of the boiling water and leave to stand for 2 minutes, then stir until dissolved.

2. Top up with the rest of the water and leave to cool briefly.

3. Fill 4 heatproof glasses with a mixture of the fruit and then pour over the prepared jelly liquid.

4. Top with a few basil leaves; cover and chill until set before serving.

Vanilla Poached Pears

Serves: 6
Preparation time: 5–10 minutes
Cooking time: 50–55 minutes
Calories/serving: 340

Ingredients

500 ml / 18 fl. oz / 2 cups water

110 g / 4 oz / ½ cup golden caster (superfine) sugar

2 vanilla pods, split lengthwise

500 ml / 18 fl. oz / 2 cups dry white wine

6 medium ripe pears, peeled

Method

1. Combine the water, sugar and vanilla pods in a large saucepan. Bring to a simmer, stirring occasionally, until the sugar dissolves.

2. Add the wine and bring to boiling point; add the pears and return to a simmer.

3. Poach for 40–45 minutes until soft to the point of a knife.

4. Leave to cool before serving.

Treats to Take Away

It can be a real challenge to stick to three meals per day, with nothing in between. And yet, traditional snack items can be the worst for dairy ingredients: chocolate bars, biscuits, crackers and cheese are obviously all no-nos.

As you perfect your dairy-free diet, you may become an expert at choosing from the limited items available at the motorway services or coffee shop, or at making sure you always have dried fruit and nuts in your bag.

Better than that, check out the mouthwatering recipes in this section and see what takes your fancy. These treats can be made in batches and stored or frozen so that you always have something handy when you head out of the house. But be careful – they are so delicious and tempting that even your dairy-friendly friends might dip in and deplete your supplies!

Tofu Cookies

Makes: 12
Preparation time: 10 minutes
Cooking time: 14–16 minutes
Calorie/serving: 78

Ingredients

110 g / 4 oz / ⅔ cup firm tofu
200 g / 7 oz / 2 cups oat bran
75 g / 3 oz / ½ cup agave nectar
a few mint leaves, finely chopped
½ tsp ground cinnamon
½ tsp baking powder
½ tsp bicarbonate of (baking) soda
a pinch of salt
110 g / 4 oz / ½ cup dairy-free
   coconut milk yoghurt
1 tsp vanilla extract

Method

1. Preheat the oven to 180°C (160°C fan) /
   350F / gas 4 and line a large baking tray
   with greaseproof paper.

2. Pulse the tofu in a food processor until
   finely chopped.

3. Tip into a bowl along with the oat bran,
   agave nectar, mint, cinnamon, baking
   powder, bicarbonate of soda and salt.

4. Stir well, then incorporate the yoghurt
   and vanilla extract until you have a rough
   cookie dough; add a little water if it seems
   too stiff.

5. Shape the mixture into rounds and arrange,
   spaced apart, on the baking tray. Bake for
   14–16 minutes until golden-brown and set
   before serving.

Stewed Cranberries

Serves: 4
Preparation time: 5 minutes
Cooking time: 20 minutes
Calories/serving: 160

Ingredients

100 g / 3 ½ oz / ½ cup caster
(superfine) sugar
250 ml / 9 fl. oz / 1 cup water
125 ml / 4 ½ fl. oz / ½ cup orange juice
450 g / 1 lb / 4 cups cranberries
1 cinnamon stick

Method

1. Combine the sugar, water and orange juice in a saucepan.
2. Bring to the boil, then reduce to a simmer and adding the cranberries.
3. Stir well and return to the boil, then reduce the heat and cook for 12–14 minutes until soft and bursting.
4. Leave to cool before serving.

Carrot Muffins

Makes: 12
Preparation time: 20–25 minutes
Cooking time: 25–30 minutes
Calories/serving: 150

Ingredients

200 g / 7 oz / 1 ⅓ cups plain
   (all-purpose) flour
1 tsp baking powder
a pinch of ground cinnamon
½ tsp salt
175 g / 6 oz / ¾ cup caster (superfine) sugar
3 large eggs
150 ml / 5 fl. oz / ⅔ cup sunflower oil
2 large carrots, peeled and grated

Method

1. Preheat the oven to 180°C (160°C fan) /
   350F / gas 4 and line a 12-hole muffin tin
   with cases.

2. Sift the flour, baking powder, cinnamon,
   salt and sugar into a mixing bowl, then stir
   well.

3. Beat together the eggs and oil in a jug;
   add to the dry ingredients and fold briefly
   to incorporate.

4. Fold through the carrot and divide the
   batter between the cases.

5. Bake for 20–25 minutes until golden and
   risen; a toothpick should come out clean
   from their centres.

6. Remove to a wire rack to cool before serving.

Buckwheat Crackers

Serves: 4
Preparation time: 15 minutes
Cooking time: 10–15 minutes
Calories/serving: 418

Ingredients

300 g / 10 ½ oz / 2 cups buckwheat flour, plus extra for dusting

55 ml / 2 fl. oz / ¼ cup sunflower oil

½ tsp salt

110 ml / 4 fl. oz / ½ cup warm water

2 tbsp sesame seeds

2 tbsp black poppy seeds

175 g / 6 oz / ¾ cup hummus, to serve

Method

1. Preheat the oven to 190°C (170°C fan) / 375F / gas 5 and line a large baking tray with greaseproof paper.

2. Mix the flour with the oil, salt and half of the water in a mixing bowl; mix in more water as necessary until you have a non-sticky dough.

3. Turn out the dough onto a floured surface and knead briefly, then roll out to ½ cm (¼ in) thickness.

4. Cut into triangles and arrange on the lined baking tray, then top with sesame and poppy seeds.

5. Bake for 10–15 minutes until golden and crisp, then remove to a wire rack to cool before serving with the hummus.

Apple Cinnamon Tartlets

Makes: 8
Preparation time: 15 minutes
Cooking time: 30–35 minutes
Calories/serving: 271

Ingredients

600 g / 1 lb 5 oz / 4 cups Bramley apples, peeled, cored and diced

125 g / 4 ½ oz / ⅔ cup soft dark brown sugar

2 tbsp water

1 cinnamon stick

250 g / 9 oz / 1 cup ready-made vegan shortcrust pastry

a little plain (all-purpose) flour, for dusting

4 golden delicious apples, peeled, cored and sliced

½ tsp ground cinnamon

Method

1. Combine the Bramley apple, sugar, water and cinnamon stick in a saucepan.

2. Cook over a medium heat until simmering; cover with a lid and cook over a reduced heat for 8–10 minutes until very soft.

3. Purée the apples in a food processor, then leave to cool.

4. Preheat the oven to 190°C (170°C fan) / 375F / gas 5 and roll out the pastry on a lightly floured surface into a round approximately ½ cm (¼ in) thick.

5. Cut 8 rounds approximately 10 cm (4 in) in diameter; lift onto a baking tray and prick with a fork.

6. Top with the apple purée and then slices of apple; bake for 18–22 minutes. Garnish with ground cinnamon.

Cinnamon-stewed Apples

Serves: 4
Preparation time: 10–15 minutes
Cooking time: 15 minutes
Calories/serving: 243

Ingredients

1 kg / 2 lb 4 oz / 6 ⅔ cups Bramley apples, peeled, cored and diced

150 g / 5 oz / ⅔ cup caster (superfine) sugar

3 tbsp hot water

1 cinnamon stick

a pinch of ground cinnamon

Method

1. Combine the apples, sugar, water and spices in a saucepan; stir well and cover with a lid.

2. Cook over a reduced heat for 12–15 minutes until very soft.

3. Once soft enough, mash into a rough purée. Leave to cool before serving in jars.

Teatime Scones

Makes: 12
Preparation time: 15 minutes
Cooking time: 12–15 minutes
Calories/serving: 131

Ingredients

75 g / 3 oz / ⅓ cup coconut oil,
  chilled and cubed

225 g / 8 oz / 1 ½ cups self-raising flour,
  plus extra for dusting

1 tbsp cornflour (cornstarch)

½ tsp salt

175 ml / 6 fl. oz / ¾ cup almond milk

1 small egg, beaten

Method

1. Preheat the oven to 190°C (170°C fan) /
   375F / gas 5 and line a large baking tray
   with greaseproof paper.

2. Pulse together the coconut oil, flour,
   cornflour and salt until they resemble
   breadcrumbs, then add the milk and mix
   well to form a soft dough.

3. Turn out the dough onto a floured surface,
   pat into a round, and roll out to 2 cm (1 in)
   thickness.

4. Use a 5 cm (2 in) round cutter to stamp out
   12 rounds before arranging, spaced apart,
   on the tray.

5. Brush the tops with beaten egg and bake
   for 12–15 minutes until golden and risen.
   Remove to a wire rack to cool completely
   before serving.

Seeded Crackers

Serves: 4
Preparation time: 20 minutes
Cooking time: 14–16 minutes
Calories/serving: 200

Ingredients

75 g / 3 oz / ½ cup plain (all-purpose) flour, plus extra for dusting

75 g / 3 oz / ½ cup buckwheat flour

½ tsp caster (superfine) sugar

½ tsp salt

1 ½ tbsp extra virgin olive oil

75 ml / 3 fl. oz / ⅓ cup warm water

1 tbsp sunflower seeds

1 tsp flaxseeds

1 tsp black poppy seeds

flaked sea salt

Method

1. Preheat the oven to 200°C (180°C fan) / 400F / gas 6 and line a couple of baking trays with greaseproof paper.

2. Combine the flours, sugar and salt in a large mixing bowl. Add the oil and water gradually, mixing until a soft, tacky dough comes together.

3. Turn out the dough on a floured surface and knead briefly, then roll out to ½ cm (¼ in) thickness.

4. Cut into squares and arrange on the baking trays, spaced apart.

5. Bake for 14–16 minutes until golden and crisp. Remove to a wire rack to cool, then garnish with seeds and sea salt before serving.

Individual Plum Clafoutis

Serves: 4
Preparation time: 15 minutes
Cooking time: 20–25 minutes
Calories/serving: 324

Ingredients

75 g / 3 oz / ½ cup plain (all-purpose)
  flour, sifted

55 g / 2 oz / ¼ cup granulated sugar

a pinch of salt

3 tbsp coconut oil

3 medium eggs

1 lemon, zested

75 ml / 3 fl. oz / ⅓ cup almond milk

400 g / 14 oz / 2 cups canned plums in juice

Method

1. Preheat the oven to 180°C (160°C fan) /
   350F / gas 4 and whisk together the flour,
   sugar and salt.

2. Whisk in the coconut oil, eggs and
   lemon zest until you have a smooth
   batter. Add the milk and continue to
   whisk for 2–3 minutes until light and fluffy.

3. Pour the batter into individual dishes and
   spoon in the plums and any juice.

4. Arrange on a baking tray and bake for
   20–25 minutes until golden and set.

5. Remove to a wire rack to cool slightly
   before serving.

Citrus Granita

Serves: 4
Preparation time:
10 minutes plus freezing
Cooking time: 10 minutes
Calories/serving: 194

Ingredients

750 ml / 1 pint 6 fl. oz / 3 cups freshly
squeezed orange juice

2 white grapefruit, juiced

75 g / 3 oz / ⅓ cup agave nectar

2 tbsp vodka

Method

1. Combine the orange juice, grapefruit juice,
   agave nectar and vodka in a saucepan.

2. Warm over a low heat, stirring until the
   agave has dissolved, then leave to cool.

3. Pour into a shallow freezer-proof dish and
   then freeze for 2 hours.

4. Remove and break up the mixture into
   slush with a fork, then return to the freezer
   for a further hour.

5. Repeat the previous step and return to the
   freezer for a further hour until set.

6. Break up the granita with a fork before
   serving in glasses.

Praline Tart Tatin

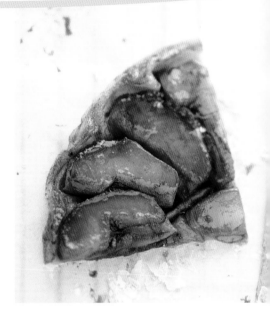

Serves: 6
Preparation time: 10–15 minutes
Cooking time: 35–40 minutes
Calories/serving: 388

Ingredients

75 g / 3 oz / ⅓ cup coconut oil

75 g / 3 oz / ⅓ cup light brown soft sugar

75 g / 3 oz / ¾ cup pecans, finely chopped

4 golden delicious apples, peeled, cored and sliced

100 g / 3 ½ oz / ½ cup ready-made vegan pastry

a little plain (all-purpose) flour, for dusting

Method

1. Preheat the oven to 200°C (180°C fan) / 400°F / gas 6. Melt the coconut oil in a tatin pan or 18 cm (7 in) sauté pan set over a moderate heat.

2. Add the sugar and cook for 2 minutes, stirring occasionally, until syrupy, then stir in the nuts.

3. Reduce the heat and add the apple to the pan, fitting as necessary.

4. Cook over a reduced heat. Roll out the pastry on a lightly floured surface into a round approximately 20 cm (8 in) in diameter, pricking with a fork.

5. Remove the pan from the heat and drape over the pastry. Tuck it in around the edges.

6. Bake for 20–25 minutes until golden, then remove and turn out. Serve warm.

Mini Chorizo Muffins

Makes: 12
Preparation time: 10 minutes
Cooking time: 22–25 minutes
Calories/serving: 140

Ingredients

1 tbsp coconut oil

275 g / 10 oz / 1 ¾ cups plain
(all-purpose) flour

1 tsp baking powder

½ tsp salt

1 medium egg

225 ml / 8 fl. oz / 1 cup almond milk

150 g / 5 oz / 1 cup mangetout, chopped

150 g / 5 oz / 1 cup chorizo, peeled and
finely diced

100 g / 3 ½ oz / 1 cup dairy-free cheese, grated

Method

1. Preheat the oven to 180°C (160°C fan) /
   350F / gas 4 and grease a 12-hole mini
   muffin tin with coconut oil.

2. Sift the flour, baking powder and salt into
   a mixing bowl, then beat together the egg
   and milk in a jug before adding to the bowl.

3. Mix briefly until the mixture starts to come
   together, then fold through the mangetout,
   chorizo and cheese.

4. Spoon into the holes and bake for 22–25
   minutes until golden and risen.

5. Remove to a wire rack to cool before
   turning out and serving.

Meal Plans and Diary

One of the hardest aspects of a dairy-free diet is being limited in your choices as you browse the shelves of the supermarket. So many items are out of bounds because of their ingredients.

The key to success is to find new, exciting substitutes for much-loved foods. Don't simply cut out essentials but replace them with alternatives that may soon become your chosen taste-bud tantalisers when you're in need of a treat. Experiment with the recipes in the previous sections so that mealtimes don't become a chore. Food is meant to be fun, as well as fuel for a healthy body, full of vitality.

Don't forget to plan

Most people find that organisation is paramount in making their dairy-free days run smoothly and easily. Take time at the weekend to flick through the recipes and fill in a meal plan for the week ahead. Choose two or three lunches and make double the amount, which will then see you through the week. Decide on your evening meals and make sure that you shop efficiently for the right ingredients so nothing is wasted.

It's important, too, that you don't deny yourself treats. The chances are that your decision to ditch dairy will be a long-term plan, so you need to know how to choose treats that fit the bill. Bake in batches and freeze any excess, so you always have something tasty for that between-meals lull, or when you're on the road. Don't ever think that dairy-free equals fun-free – it's up to you how much you enjoy your food!

Week 1

	Breakfast	Lunch	Dinner	Snacks
Monday				
Tuesday				
Wednesday				
Thursday				
Friday				
Saturday				
Sunday				

How I feel (at the start of the week)

Improvements felt during the week

Symptoms I'm aiming to clear

New foods tried

Week 2

	Breakfast	Lunch	Dinner	Snacks
Monday				
Tuesday				
Wednesday				
Thursday				
Friday				
Saturday				
Sunday				

How I feel (at the start of the week)

Improvements felt during the week

Symptoms I'm aiming to clear

New foods tried

Week 3

	Breakfast	Lunch	Dinner	Snacks
Monday				
Tuesday				
Wednesday				
Thursday				
Friday				
Saturday				
Sunday				

How I feel (at the start of the week)

Improvements felt during the week

Symptoms I'm aiming to clear

New foods tried

Week 4

	Breakfast	Lunch	Dinner	Snacks
Monday				
Tuesday				
Wednesday				
Thursday				
Friday				
Saturday				
Sunday				

How I feel (at the start of the week)

Improvements felt during the week

Symptoms I'm aiming to clear

New foods tried

Shopping List

To begin with, you will find that you need to refill your cupboards with a selection of new, dairy-free items. Plan your meals and make a list as you go along, buying new store-cupboard essentials as well as the staple ingredients for your chosen recipes.

Store-cupboard items

Cooking oil – sunflower, olive, rapeseed, coconut

Dairy-free chocolate

Carob powder, solid chocolate

Cocoa (cacao) powder (pure/raw)

Honey and syrup (maple, agave nectar, molasses)

Polenta (a good alternative to breadcrumbs)

Quinoa (high in calcium)

Millet (high in protein)

Beans – aduki, black-eyed, borlotti, butter, cannellini, haricot (good for adding creaminess and texture)

Lentils and chickpeas (garbanzo beans)

Dried mushrooms

Tinned fish

Seeds – pumpkin, sunflower, sesame, linseed

Nuts – all types, unless you're allergic

Passata

Pasta

Noodles

Rice (brown, white, basmati, arborio)

Garlic

Spices

Herbs

Tomato purée

Cornflour (cornstarch)

Stock cubes

Flour

Fridge/freezer and other items

Dairy-free milk/cream – soya, nut, rice

Dairy-free spread – sunflower, soya

Nut butter – peanut, almond, cashew

Dairy-free yoghurt, cream, cheese,
    ice cream

Meat

Fish

Seafood

Tofu

Eggs

Vegetables

Potatoes

Fruit

Dairy-free biscuits

Dairy-free breadcrumbs

Root ginger

Lemongrass

Tahini

Fail-safe Food Guide

At first, shopping will be a time-consuming task as you scour the ingredients lists for pitfalls. Keep a note here of tried-and-trusted products to save yourself valuable minutes on each trip. Note down items that have caught you out with hidden milk-based products, too. But always remember to revisit the items periodically in case the recipe or preparation conditions change.

Free-from items

No-go items

Dairy-free ME!

So, how is it going? Are you reaping the benefits of a fresh and healthy diet, without any of the symptoms that prompted you to ditch dairy in the first place?

As you explore and experiment with the recipes in this book, you should find that you grow in confidence and enjoy the whole experience of eating so much more – especially without the fear of adverse side effects after a meal or a treat. Maybe you have extended the dairy-free diet to your whole family so that you can cook one meal for all, leaving your loved ones also feeling brighter and lighter. The next step is to share your culinary creations with friends and see if they even notice the absence of dairy ingredients.

A new lifestyle

The joy of the whole process is that there is no 'point of return', where you wonder what you're missing – because you aren't missing anything. With luck, you won't feel the need to reintroduce dairy produce, but if you do, take tiny steps and monitor your body's reaction after each new food. Be prepared to knock out items at the first sign of unwanted feelings of tiredness, worsening of your skin or stomach problems.

After a while, you should have a newfound love of food in all its glory, with far fewer processed and packaged products. You will discover that there is no room in your food diary for dairy items, as you are now buying, cooking and eating so many new or forgotten foods that had been forced out of your meal plans. It's a whole new you!